Fast
Chicken

KÖNEMANN

Chicken basics

Choosing and storing your chicken are just as important as preparation and will guarantee a really tasty and healthy meal.

❖ ❖ ❖

Getting a freshly prepared meal on the table in just 30 minutes can be quite a challenge, especially when it needs to be cooked as thoroughly as chicken. But a simple checklist can make it seem effortless.

A thigh fillet, drumstick and breast fillet.

Buying. Try to choose chicken pieces with flesh that looks light pink and moist. If you are buying frozen, make sure it is solid and tightly wrapped. Free-range or corn-fed chickens tend to be smaller but are well worth buying as they usually have more flavour.

It is a good idea to put chicken down as the last item to buy on your shopping list to minimise the time it is out of the refrigerator.

Storage. Once you get home, transfer the chicken from its plastic wrap to a plate and cover it with foil before placing in your refrigerator. This will keep the meat moist and fresh. Label and date the chicken and cook it within 2 days of purchasing.

Barbecued chickens need to be taken out of the bag and left to cool

Shred the meat from the barbecued chicken.

slightly before you shred the meat from them. Store in the refrigerator if you are not using straight away.

Freezing chicken in small portions gives you the freedom to defrost a few pieces at a time as you need them. The best way to defrost chicken is to place it on a plate or tray and leave to thaw in the refrigerator, allowing 3 hours for each 500 g (1 lb).

Frozen chicken pieces or fillets can also be thawed in the microwave on the defrost setting, but this is not recommended for whole chickens, as the thawing is uneven and parts of the bird begin to cook before other parts are fully defrosted. Never refreeze chicken, and always cook it within 12 hours of thawing. Cooked chicken can be kept in the refrigerator for up to 3 days.

Preparation. Breast fillets are usually sold as a whole breast that has been skinned and removed from the

Cut the double breast into two single fillets.

bone. These can be separated into two single fillets. The recipes in this book use single fillets (each weighing about 200 g/ 6 1/2 oz) that have had the tenderloin removed.

The tenderloin runs along the back of the breast fillet and can be easily pulled off. Keep it to use in a stir-fry.

Remove the tenderloin from the back of the fillet.

Remove any excess fat or sinew from the fillet and, if you choose to leave the tenderloin on, discard the tough

Remove the membrane from the tenderloin.

white membrane at the top by holding the tip of the fillet and gently scraping it away with a sharp knife.

To cut down on cooking time, you can flatten breast and thigh fillets between 2 sheets

Flatten the fillet between 2 sheets of plastic wrap.

of plastic wrap or score them with a sharp knife. With drumsticks, make a couple of deep slashes at the top of each one. This will also assist in even cooking.

To test if chicken is cooked, insert a skewer into the thickest part of the meat. If the juices run clear, the chicken is ready. If the juices are pink, it needs a little more time. Breast fillets with the tenderloin still on may take a little longer to cook than the time given.

Making stock. Rather than discarding a barbecued or roast chicken carcass, why not use it to make chicken stock. Place the carcass in a large pan with a bouquet garni, 2 chopped onions, 2 roughly chopped carrots and 2 sticks of

celery, including the leaves. Cover with 3 litres of water, bring to the boil and simmer slowly for 3 hours, skimming off any froth with a large spoon if necessary.

Strain the stock through a fine sieve and then freeze it by putting

Strain the stock, reserving the liquid.

a plastic bag inside a measuring jug and pouring in the liquid. That way you can measure how much stock you have. When frozen, remove the bag from the jug, and seal securely before placing back in the freezer. Alternatively, pour the stock straight into ice cube trays and freeze.

Pour the stock into ice cube trays and freeze.

Fast Chicken

If you want chicken tonight without reaching for the bottled sauce, try one of these quick tasty recipes for a satisfying meal.

Chicken with Brazil Nut Butter

Ready to eat in
30 minutes
Serves 4

1/2 cup (80 g/2²/3 oz) brazil nuts, toasted
1 fresh red chilli, seeded and finely chopped
90 g (3 oz) butter, softened
2 tablespoons finely chopped fresh basil
4 chicken breast fillets
1 tablespoon freshly squeezed lemon juice
2 tablespoons olive oil

1. Place the brazil nuts, chilli and butter in a food processor or blender and process until combined. Transfer to a bowl and stir in the basil. Cover and refrigerate until just before serving.
2. Slash the chicken fillets deeply 3–4 times diagonally across the top. Place in a dish and coat with the lemon juice and 1 tablespoon of the oil.
3. Heat the remaining oil in a heavy-based pan. Add the chicken and cook for 3–4 minutes each side, turning once, or until cooked through. Brush a few times with the marinade during cooking. Cut each fillet into 3–4 slices.
4. Serve the chicken slices with couscous and salad, with a spoonful of the Brazil Nut Butter.

NUTRITION PER SERVE
Protein 30 g; Fat 45 g; Carbohydrate 1 g; Dietary Fibre 2 g; Cholesterol 115 mg; 2160 kJ (515 cal)

Note: Add flavour to instant couscous by stirring through 2 tablespoons finely chopped fresh parsley, 2 teaspoons grated lemon rind and 20 g (²/3 oz) butter just before serving. Season with salt and pepper.

Chicken with Brazil Nut Butter

Peppered Chicken and Vegetables

*Ready to eat in
  30 minutes
Serves 4*

5 chicken thigh fillets
  (600 g/1 1/4 lb)
1/2 teaspoon green
  peppercorns
2 tablespoons oil
20 g (2/3 oz) butter
2 cloves garlic, chopped
1 large carrot, chopped
2 celery sticks, sliced
3 tablespoons white
  wine
2 tablespoons cream
2 bay leaves

1. Roughly dice the
chicken. Crush the
peppercorns with the
back of a spoon and set
aside. Heat the oil and
butter in a large pan.
Cook the chicken and
garlic over high heat in
batches for about
3 minutes, or until the
chicken is browned.
2. Reduce the heat and
add the carrot and
celery. Toss well, cover
and cook for 3 minutes.
Add the wine, cream,
peppercorns and bay
leaves. Cook, covered,
for a further 5 minutes.
Season and remove the
bay leaves.

NUTRITION PER SERVE
*Protein 30 g; Fat 25 g;
Carbohydrate 2 g; Dietary
Fibre 1 g; Cholesterol
130 mg; 1530 kJ (365 cal)*

Note: Buy green
peppercorns in small
cans or jars from
supermarkets and
delicatessens.

Chicken and Prawn Laksa

*Ready to eat in
  30 minutes
Serves 4–6*

2 tablespoons oil
2 teaspoons grated
  fresh ginger
2 cloves garlic, crushed
8 spring onions, sliced
8 chicken tenderloins,
  sliced
2–3 tablespoons mild
  curry paste
3 cups (750 ml/24 fl oz)
  hot chicken stock
1 1/2 cups (375 ml/
  12 fl oz) coconut milk
12 small raw prawns,
  peeled, tails intact
150 g (5 oz) Chinese
  vermicelli
50 g (1 2/3 oz) snow
  peas, halved
100 g (3 1/3 oz) bean
  sprouts
1/3 cup (20 g/2/3 oz)
  chopped fresh mint
1/3 cup (20 g/2/3 oz)
  chopped fresh
  coriander

1. Heat the oil in a
wok. Add the ginger,
garlic and spring onion;
stir-fry for 1 minute.

Add the tenderloins to
the wok and stir-fry for
a further 2–3 minutes,
or until just cooked.
Stir in the curry paste
until the chicken is
well coated.
2. Add the hot chicken
stock and stir in the
coconut milk. Bring
slowly to the boil, then
reduce the heat and
simmer for 3 minutes.
Add the prawns and
simmer for a further
3 minutes.
3. Meanwhile, place the
vermicelli in a large
heatproof bowl and
pour over enough
boiling water to cover.
Set aside for 5 minutes,
or until soft. Drain the
vermicelli and divide
among large, warmed
serving bowls. Add the
snow peas and some
bean sprouts, then ladle
over the hot laksa.
Serve sprinkled with
mint, coriander and
the remaining
bean sprouts.

NUTRITION PER SERVE (6)
*Protein 40 g; Fat 35 g;
Carbohydrate 10 g; Dietary
Fibre 2 g; Cholesterol
110 mg; 2090 kJ (500 cal)*

Note: Peanut oil is
most suitable for
Asian cooking as it
withstands higher
cooking temperatures.

*Peppered Chicken and Vegetables (top)
with Chicken and Prawn Laksa*

Poached Chicken and Ricotta Meatballs

*Ready to eat in
30 minutes
Serves 4*

350 g (11¼ oz) fine
  chicken mince
100 g (3⅓ oz) fresh
  ricotta
¼ cup (35 g/1¼ oz)
  chopped black olives
2 teaspoons grated
  lemon rind
2 teaspoons chopped
  fresh oregano
1½ cups (375 ml/
  12 fl oz) pasta sauce
1 cup (250 ml/8 fl oz)
  chicken stock
1 teaspoon soft
  brown sugar
2 teaspoons cornflour

1. Combine the mince, ricotta, olives, rind and oregano in a bowl. Season with salt and pepper. Knead the mixture with your fingertips for 2 minutes until well combined. With wet hands, roll quickly into small meatballs about the size of a walnut.
2. Heat the pasta sauce, stock and sugar in a large frying pan. Add the meatballs and bring to a slow boil. Simmer very gently for about 6 minutes, turning the meatballs over in the sauce a few times, until just firm.
3. Season the sauce with salt and pepper. Combine the cornflour with 1 tablespoon water. Stir in the cornflour mixture and cook until the sauce boils and thickens. Spoon the sauce over the meatballs and serve with pasta.

NUTRITION PER SERVE
*Protein 25 g; Fat 10 g;
Carbohydrate 15 g; Dietary
Fibre 3 g; Cholesterol
70 mg; 915 kJ (220 cal)*

Thai-style Chicken with Coriander Mango Salsa

*Ready to eat in
30 minutes
Serves 4–6*

2 tablespoons oil
1 clove garlic, finely
  chopped
1 teaspoon grated fresh
  ginger
500 g (1 lb) chicken
  tenderloins, sliced
1 tablespoon light soy
  sauce
½ teaspoon grated
  palm sugar (or soft
  brown sugar)
2 tablespoons sweet
  chilli sauce
2 tablespoons fish sauce
2 tablespoons lime juice
150 g (4¾ oz) fresh
  Hokkien noodles
½ bunch Chinese
  broccoli

Coriander Mango Salsa
1 small red onion,
  finely chopped
¼ cup chopped fresh
  coriander
200 g (6½ oz) mango,
  finely diced
2 tablespoons red wine
  vinegar

1. Heat the oil in a pan. Add the garlic and ginger and cook over moderate heat for 1 minute.
2. Add the chicken and brown for 4–5 minutes. Add the soy, sugar, sweet chilli and fish sauces and lime juice. Simmer for 3 minutes, or until the chicken is cooked.
3. Meanwhile, cook the noodles in boiling water until tender. Drain, add to the pan, along with the broccoli, and toss well. Serve with the Coriander Mango Salsa.
4. **To make Coriander Mango Salsa:** Combine all the ingredients in a bowl and mix well.

NUTRITION PER SERVE (6)
*Protein 25 g; Fat 9 g;
Carbohydrate 15 g; Dietary
Fibre 2 g; Cholesterol
40 mg; 955 kJ (230 cal)*

*Poached Chicken and Ricotta Meatballs (top) and
Thai-style Chicken with Coriander Mango Salsa*

Smoked Chicken Salad with Japanese Dressing

Thinly slice 3 smoked chicken breast fillets. Cut 1 small cucumber, carrot and celery stick into matchsticks. Blanch the carrot and celery for 1 minute in boiling water, then plunge into cold water and drain. Combine the chicken, cucumber, carrot and celery. Mix in 4 sliced shiitake mushrooms, 1/4 cup (15 g/1/2 oz) chopped fresh coriander and 3 tablespoons Japanese pickled ginger.

To make Japanese Dressing: Gently heat 2 tablespoons oil, 1/3 cup (80 ml/2 3/4 fl oz) mirin, 1 tablespoon horseradish cream, 2 teaspoons light soy sauce and 1/2 teaspoon sesame oil in a pan. Whisk to combine, then pour the dressing over the salad and sprinkle lightly with 2 tablespoons lightly toasted sesame seeds. *Ready to eat in 30 minutes. Serves 6*

NUTRITION PER SERVE
Protein 15 g; Fat 15 g; Carbohydrate 5 g; Dietary Fibre 2 g; Cholesterol 30 mg; 1000 kJ (240 cal)

Pan-fried Chicken with Vinegar

Cut 4 chicken breast fillets in half horizontally. Heat 25 g (3/4 oz) butter in a large, heavy-based pan. Add chicken breast fillets and cook over medium high heat for 4 minutes on each side. Pour 1/3 cup (80 ml/ 2 3/4 fl oz) balsamic vinegar into the pan. Bring to the boil. Turn the chicken so it is well coated in the balsamic vinegar. Sprinkle 2 tablespoons of chopped fresh parsley over

the chicken. Slice the chicken into strips and serve. Garnish with salad leaves and accompany with vegetables if desired. Grilled potatoes are also a perfect accompaniment.
Ready to eat in 20 minutes. Serves 4

NUTRITION PER SERVE
Protein 25 g; Fat 15 g; Carbohydrate 2 g; Dietary Fibre 0 g; Cholesterol 90 mg; 960 kJ (230 cal)

From left to right: Smoked Chicken Salad with Japanese Dressing; Pan-fried Chicken with Vinegar; Pesto Chicken Pasta

Pesto Chicken Pasta

Cook 250 g (8 oz) spiral pasta in a large pan of boiling water until tender; drain. Meanwhile, remove the skin and meat from a barbecued chicken. Chop into bite-sized pieces and place in a large bowl. Add 1 cup (125 g/4 oz) toasted, roughly chopped walnuts. Grill 4 bacon rashers until crisp; cool and roughly chop. Add the bacon, 250 g (8 oz) halved cherry tomatoes and 60 g (2 oz) pitted and sliced Kalamata olives to the chicken mixture. Add the pasta, 1/2 cup (125 g/4 oz) ready-made pesto and 1/2 cup (30 g/1 oz) shredded fresh basil. Toss together well and serve with Parmesan shavings, if desired.
Ready to eat in 30 minutes. Serves 4

NUTRITION PER SERVE
Protein 55 g; Fat 45 g; Carbohydrate 25 g; Dietary Fibre 5 g; Cholesterol 190 mg; 3005 kJ (715 cal)

Chicken Burritos

*Ready to eat in
  30 minutes
Serves 4*

Chicken Filling
2 cans 425g (13¹/2 oz)
  tomatoes, roughly
  chopped
1 tablespoon olive oil
2 onions, diced
2 cloves garlic, crushed
¹/2–1 teaspoon chilli
  powder
¹/2 teaspoon cumin
2 cups (350 g/11¹/4 oz)
  shredded, cooked
  chicken

8 flour tortillas
2 cups (130 g/4¹/4 oz)
  shredded lettuce
  leaves
4 tomatoes, sliced
1 small red onion,
  finely sliced
1 cup (125 g/4 oz)
  grated Cheddar cheese

**1. To make Chicken
Filling:** Preheat the
oven to moderately hot
200°C (400°F/Gas 6).
Drain off half the liquid
from the canned
tomatoes. Heat the oil
in a large frying pan
and cook the onion and
garlic until soft. Add
the chilli, cumin and
tomatoes and season to
taste. Simmer for
6 minutes, or until
most of the liquid has
evaporated. Stir in the
shredded chicken and

place in a bowl. Cover
and keep warm.
2. Meanwhile, wrap the
tortillas in foil and
warm in the oven for
10 minutes. Place the
chicken mixture on the
centre of the burritos.
Arrange the lettuce,
tomato, onion and
cheese on top of the
mixture and roll up.
Alternatively, serve the
fillings in separate
bowls and let people
make up their own.

NUTRITION PER SERVE
*Protein 30 g; Fat 15 g;
Carbohydrate 40 g; Dietary
Fibre 4 g; Cholesterol
95 mg; 1840 kJ (440 cal)*

Note: Use a barbecued
chicken, leftover roast
chicken or cooked
chicken breast fillets.
Be sure to keep the
tortillas warm, as they
become dry and crusty
when cold. Once the
burritos are rolled,
wrap in paper napkins
to keep moist. Tortillas
may also be heated in
the microwave. Heat
on High (100%) for
1 minute, or until hot
and steamy.
Variation: Add some
guacamole as one of
the fillings and shake a
little Tabasco sauce
over the burrito before
rolling up.

Chicken with Mozzarella Basil Stuffing
*Ready to eat in
  25 minutes
Serves 4*

4 chicken breast fillets
2 teaspoons Dijon
  mustard
4 slices mozzarella
4 large fresh basil leaves
light olive oil
125 g (4 oz) pesto

1. Flatten the chicken
fillets between 2 sheets
of plastic wrap until
2 cm (³/4 inch) thick,
using a rolling pin or
meat mallet. Cut a
pocket in each fillet and
spread ¹/4 teaspoon
Dijon mustard around
the cavity. In each
cavity place a slice of
mozzarella and a large
basil leaf. Secure with
toothpicks.
2. Heat some light olive
oil in a frying pan.
Cook chicken over
moderate heat for
4–6 minutes each side,
until cooked through.
Remove the toothpicks,
slice and serve hot with
pesto and roast tomatoes.

NUTRITION PER SERVE
*Protein 35 g; Fat 30 g;
Carbohydrate 5 g; Dietary
Fibre 1 g; Cholesterol
80 mg; 1730 kJ (415 cal)*

*Chicken Burritos (top)
and Chicken with Mozzarella Basil Stuffing*

Chicken Salad with Blue Cheese

*Ready to eat in
30 minutes
Serves 4*

Caesar Dressing
1 egg
2 teaspoons white wine
vinegar
3 teaspoons Dijon
mustard
1 clove garlic, crushed
1/3 cup oil

1 barbecued chicken
2 cups (360 g/11 1/2 oz)
grapes
1 cup (100 g/3 1/3 oz)
snow pea sprouts
1/2 cup (50 g/1 2/3 oz)
pecans
mixed salad leaves,
washed, to serve
75 g (2 1/2 oz) blue
cheese, crumbled
3/4 cup (25 g/3/4 oz)
ready-made croutons

1. To make Caesar Dressing: Place the egg, vinegar, Dijon mustard and garlic in a food processor or blender and process until smooth. With the motor running, gradually add the oil in a thin stream. Blend until well combined.
2. Remove the skin and meat from the chicken. Roughly shred and combine in a bowl with the grapes, snow pea sprouts, pecans and Caesar dressing. Toss the salad lightly until well combined.
3. Line a large bowl with the mixed salad leaves; fill with the chicken salad and garnish with the crumbled blue cheese and the croutons.

NUTRITION PER SERVE
Protein 40 g; Fat 40 g;
Carbohydrate 50 g; Dietary
Fibre 5 g; Cholesterol
165 mg; 2900 kJ (690 cal)

Grilled Chicken Kebabs with Chilli Fruit Salsa

*Ready to eat in
25 minutes
Serves 4*

2 red capsicums, cubed
4 chicken breast fillets,
cubed
4 bacon rashers, thickly
sliced
light olive oil

Chilli Fruit Salsa
2 peaches, stones
removed and roughly
diced
1/2 cup (125 g/4 oz)
plain yoghurt
juice of 2 limes
finely grated rind of
1 lime
1/3 cup (20 g/2/3 oz)
chopped fresh
coriander
1 jalapeño chilli, seeded
and chopped

1. Preheat the grill. Thread the capsicum, chicken and bacon onto 4 long metal skewers. Brush the kebabs with the light olive oil, then place under the grill. Cook, turning frequently, for about 10 minutes, or until the kebabs are cooked through and golden all over. Serve with the Fruit Salsa.
2. To make Chilli Fruit Salsa: Combine all the salsa ingredients in a bowl. Refrigerate until needed.

NUTRITION PER SERVE
Protein 60 g; Fat 8 g;
Carbohydrate 7 g; Dietary
Fibre 1.5 g; Cholesterol
135 mg; 1475 kJ (350 cal)

Note: Do not pack the kebab ingredients onto the skewers too tightly or the chicken will have trouble cooking through. This recipe is also delicious cooked on the barbecue: preheat the grill plate and brush with oil before cooking. In the Chilli Fruit Salsa, a small pawpaw can be used instead of the mango, depending on what fruit is in season.

*Chicken Salad with Blue Cheese (top) and Grilled
Chicken Kebabs with Chilli Fruit Salsa*

Chicken with Tomato and Basil Sauce

Cut 6 chicken thigh fillets into quarters. Slice a red onion into rings and roughly chop 4 bacon rashers. Heat 1 tablespoon olive oil in a large, heavy-based pan, add the chicken pieces and cook over moderate-high heat for 4–5 minutes. Set aside. Reduce the heat and add 1 tablespoon olive oil. Add the onion, bacon and 2–3 crushed cloves garlic and cook for 5 minutes, until the bacon is browned. Add 425 g (13^1/2 oz) can of chopped tomatoes. Stir in ^{1}/2 teaspoon each of dried basil and oregano and 1 teaspoon caster sugar. Cook over moderate heat for 4–5 minutes, until slightly reduced. Return the chicken to the pan and simmer for 10 minutes, turning once. Add 12 Kalamata olives and sprinkle with ^{1}/4 cup (15 g/^{1}/2 oz) chopped fresh basil. *Ready to eat in 30 minutes. Serves 4*

NUTRITION PER SERVE
Protein 40 g; Fat 20 g; Carbohydrate 10 g; Dietary Fibre 5 g; Cholesterol 120 mg; 1485 kJ (355 cal)

Thai-style Chicken Cakes

Place 500 g (1 lb) chicken mince, 1 egg and 1 tablespoon cornflour in a bowl and mix well to combine. Add 2 teaspoons red curry paste, 2 finely chopped spring onions, ^{1}/2 cup (60 g/2 oz) finely sliced green beans, ^{1}/4 cup (15 g/^{1}/2 oz) chopped fresh coriander and 1 finely chopped fresh red chilli (optional). Mix with clean hands until combined. Using wet hands, roll 2 tablespoon portions

into balls. Flatten to round patties about 8 cm (3 inches) in diameter. Add 5 cm (1/4 inch) oil to a heavy-based pan. Cook chicken cakes in batches for 5 minutes each side, or until cooked through. Don't let the oil get too hot as the patties burn easily. Drain on paper towels; serve with sweet chilli sauce.
Ready to eat in 30 minutes. Makes 12

NUTRITION PER SERVE
Protein 30 g; Fat 10 g; Carbohydrate 5 g; Dietary Fibre 1 g; Cholesterol 130 mg; 830 kJ (200 cal)

Chicken with Lemon, Parsley and Orecchiette

Add 375 g (12 oz) orecchiette to a large pan of boiling water and cook until tender; drain. Meanwhile, heat 1 tablespoon oil and 30 g (1 oz) butter in a large, heavy-based pan. Add 4 chicken breast fillets and cook for 4–5 minutes each side; slice and set aside. Stir in 1/4 cup (60 ml/ 2 fl oz) lemon juice, 3/4 cup (185 ml/6 fl oz) chicken stock and 1 cup (250 ml/8 fl oz) cream. Bring to the boil and simmer for 8 minutes. Return the sliced fillets to the pan; add 1/4 cup (15 g/ 1/2 oz) fresh chopped parsley. Divide the pasta among heated serving plates. Top with the chicken and sauce. Garnish with lemon slices and chopped fresh parsley.
Ready to eat in 30 minutes. Serves 4

NUTRITION PER SERVE
Protein 45 g; Fat 25 g; Carbohydrate 65 g; Dietary Fibre 5 g; Cholesterol 125 mg; 2860 kJ (685 cal)

Note: Orecchiette means little ears.

From left to right: Chicken with Tomato and Basil Sauce; Thai-style Chicken Cakes; Chicken with Lemon, Parsley and Orecchiette

Sesame Chicken and Vegetable Stir-fry

Ready to eat in 30 minutes
Serves 4

2 tablespoons light soy
  sauce
2 tablespoons sherry
1 tablespoon grated
  fresh ginger
1–2 cloves garlic,
  crushed
1 teaspoon soft brown
  sugar
2 teaspoons sesame oil
3 chicken breast fillets,
  thinly sliced
6 spring onions
1 red capsicum
1 zucchini
1 small carrot
1 celery stick
2 tablespoons oil
1 tablespoon sesame
  seeds, toasted

1. In a large bowl, combine the soy sauce, sherry, ginger, garlic, sugar and 1 teaspoon of the sesame oil. Add the chicken; set aside. Slice the spring onions, dice the capsicum and thinly slice the zucchini, carrot and celery.
2. Drain the chicken, reserving the marinade. Pat the chicken dry with paper towels.
3. Heat 1 tablespoon of the oil and the remaining sesame oil in a wok. Add the vegetables; stir-fry for 2–3 minutes and set aside. Heat the remaining oil, add the chicken and stir-fry for 3–4 minutes, or until just cooked. Return the vegetables to the wok with the reserved marinade. Stir-fry for 2–3 minutes. Top with sesame seeds.

NUTRITION PER SERVE
Protein 30 g; Fat 15 g; Carbohydrate 10 g; Dietary Fibre 3 g; Cholesterol 60 mg; 1305 kJ (310 cal)

Chicken with Prosciutto and Bean Purée

Ready to eat in 30 minutes
Serves 4

4 chicken breast fillets
2 tablespoons olive oil
1 tablespoon freshly
  squeezed lemon juice
1 tablespoon chopped
  fresh rosemary
4 slices prosciutto

Bean Purée
400 g (12²/3 oz) can
  cannellini beans,
  drained (see note)
2 teaspoons chopped
  fresh rosemary
2 cloves garlic, crushed
2 tablespoons cream

1. Slash the chicken breasts 3–4 times diagonally across the surface. Place in a dish and coat with the combined oil, juice and rosemary. Set aside.
2. **To make Bean Purée:** Process the beans, rosemary and garlic in a food processor or blender for 15 seconds. With the motor running, add the cream. Process until smooth. Transfer to a pan and heat gently until warm.
3. Heat a little extra oil in a heavy-based pan. Add the chicken and cook for 3–4 minutes each side, turning once, until cooked through. Brush 2–3 times with the marinade during cooking. Remove the chicken, then wrap a slice of prosciutto around each fillet. Return to the pan and cook for a further 1–2 minutes, turning once. Serve with warmed Bean Purée.

NUTRITION PER SERVE
Protein 50 g; Fat 20 g; Carbohydrate 20 g; Dietary Fibre 2 g; Cholesterol 105 mg; 1985 kJ (475 cal)

Note: Cannellini beans can be replaced with canned chick peas and a little lemon juice.

Sesame Chicken and Vegetable Stir-fry (top) and Chicken with Prosciutto and Bean Purée

Herbed Chicken with Tomato Caper Sambal

*Ready to eat in
  30 minutes
Serves 4*

16 chicken tenderloins
1 teaspoon ground
  sweet paprika
1 teaspoon dried thyme
1 teaspoon dried
  oregano
pinch of chilli powder
1/2 teaspoon freshly
  ground black pepper
1 tablespoon olive oil
1 tablespoon freshly
  squeezed lemon juice

Tomato Caper Sambal
4 large firm tomatoes,
  chopped
1 tablespoon baby
  capers
1 small red onion,
  finely chopped
1 clove garlic, crushed
2 teaspoons finely
  chopped fresh thyme
2 teaspoons finely
  chopped fresh
  oregano
1/2 teaspoon freshly
  ground black pepper

1. Cut the tenderloins in half and place them in a large dish. Mix the paprika, thyme, oregano, chilli powder and pepper in a small bowl. Stir in the olive oil and lemon juice to form a paste and coat the chicken with the paste. Set aside.
2. To make Tomato Caper Sambal: Combine all the ingredients in a bowl. Set aside.
3. Heat a little oil in a heavy-based pan; add the tenderloins. Cook for 2–3 minutes each side, turning once, until cooked through. Serve with Tomato Caper Sambal.

NUTRITION PER SERVE
*Protein 75 g; Fat 15 g;
Carbohydrate 5 g; Dietary
Fibre 5 g; Cholesterol
160 mg; 1970 kJ (470 cal)*

Mango Chicken Salad

*Ready to eat in
  30 minutes
Serves 4*

4 chicken breast fillets
2 teaspoons olive oil
2 celery sticks, diced
80 g (2³/4 oz)
  sun-dried capsicum,
  chopped
2 green capsicums,
  diced
1 small fresh red chilli,
  seeded and chopped
1 large mango, diced
2 tablespoons chopped
  mint
1/2 cup (80 g/2²/3 oz)
  unsalted macadamia
  nuts, lightly toasted
  and chopped
mixed salad leaves

Dressing
1/2 cup (125 g/4 oz)
  whole egg mayonnaise
1 teaspoon curry
  powder
3/4 cup (185 g/6 oz)
  plain yoghurt
1 tablespoon chutney

1. Preheat the oven to hot 210°C (415°F/ Gas 6–7). Place the chicken fillets in a single layer in an ovenproof dish and lightly brush with the oil. Cover with a sheet of foil and bake for 15–20 minutes, or until just cooked. Cool slightly, then cut into bite-sized pieces.
2. To make Dressing: Combine all dressing ingredients in a small bowl and mix.
3. Combine the celery, capsicums and chilli in a large bowl. Add the chicken pieces and mix. Pour over enough dressing to moisten the salad. Gently fold through the mango and the chopped mint. Serve the salad with the salad leaves and sprinkle with the macadamia nuts.

NUTRITION PER SERVE
*Protein 45 g; Fat 35 g;
Carbohydrate 25 g; Dietary
Fibre 4 g; Cholesterol
95 mg; 2380 kJ (570 cal)*

*Herbed Chicken with Tomato Caper Sambal (top)
with Mango Chicken Salad*

Chicken and Salad Souvlaki

Shred the skin and meat from a barbecued chicken and set aside. Rinse 100 g (3¹/3 oz) mixed salad leaves, including some rocket and set aside. Cut 4 small tomatoes into wedges. Cut 100 g (3¹/3 oz) feta cheese into cubes. Place the tomato, feta and 8 pitted Kalamata olives in a bowl. Whisk together 1 tablespoon each of olive oil and balsamic vinegar, lots of freshly ground black pepper and 1 teaspoon dried oregano in a jug. Pour over the tomato mixture and stir gently. Combine 1–2 crushed garlic cloves and ¹/2 cup (125 g/4 oz) whole egg mayonnaise in a bowl and spread the mixture over 4 large pitta breads. Divide the chicken, and the salad leaves among the pitta breads. Place some tomato mixture on top. Roll up firmly, tie with string and wrap in foil to serve. *Ready to eat in 30 minutes. Makes 8*

NUTRITION PER SERVE
Protein 25 g; Fat 15 g; Carbohydrate 20 g; Dietary Fibre 2 g; Cholesterol 105 mg; 1390 kJ (330 cal)

Cream of Chicken Soup

Remove the meat from a barbecued chicken; cover and refrigerate. Heat 60 g (2 oz) butter in a large, heavy-based pan. Add 1 chopped onion and 1 finely diced celery stick, carrot and parsnip. Cook over low heat, stirring, for 5 minutes. Add 3 tablespoons plain flour and cook, stirring, for 2 minutes. Slowly add 4 cups (1 litre) chicken stock, stirring until thickened. Slowly bring to the

From left to right: Chicken and Salad Souvlaki; Cream of Chicken Soup; Honey Chicken Kebabs

boil. Boil gently for 1–2 minutes, reduce the heat and simmer for 10 minutes, or until the vegetables are cooked. Add the chicken meat, 1 cup (250 ml/8 fl oz) cream, 1/2 cup (125 ml/4 fl oz) milk and 1/3 cup (20 g/ 2/3 oz) finely chopped fresh parsley. Heat gently, without boiling. Season with salt and pepper, to taste.
Ready to eat in 30 minutes. Serves 4–6

NUTRITION PER SERVE (6)
Protein 30 g; Fat 35 g; Carbohydrate 15 g; Dietary Fibre 2 g; Cholesterol 195 mg; 1955 kJ (465 cal)

Honey Chicken Kebabs

Cut 4 chicken breast fillets into chunks. Combine 1/4 cup (60 ml/2 fl oz) olive oil, 1–2 crushed cloves garlic, 2 teaspoons grated fresh ginger and 2 tablespoons each of honey, soy sauce and plum sauce in a bowl. Cut 2 zucchini and 1 red capsicum into chunks. Thread the chicken, zucchini and capsicum onto 8 metal skewers. Lay on a flat tray and brush with the marinade. Cook under a preheated grill or on a barbecue flatplate for 8 minutes, or until cooked through. Turn the skewers frequently and brush often with the marinade.
Ready to eat in 30 minutes. Makes 8

NUTRITION PER SERVE
Protein 20 g; Fat 10 g; Carbohydrate 10 g; Dietary Fibre 1 g; Cholesterol 40 mg; 835 kJ (200 cal)

Hint: If you are using bamboo skewers for this recipe, soak them for 30 minutes in a bowl of cold water and drain. This will stop them burning while the kebabs are cooking.

Green Bean and Chicken Salad

*Ready to eat in
15 minutes
Serves 4*

Vinaigrette
*1/2 cup (125 ml/4 fl oz)
light olive oil
1/4 cup (60 ml/2 fl oz)
red wine vinegar
2 tablespoons
wholegrain mustard
2 spring onions, finely
chopped
salt and freshly ground
black pepper, to taste*

*750 g (1 1/2 lb) green
beans, topped and
tailed (see note)
2 cups (350 g/11 1/4 oz)
cooked chicken,
skinned, boned and
shredded
1 punnet (250 g/8 oz)
cherry tomatoes,
halved
200 g (6 1/2 oz) Gruyère
cheese, diced*

1. To make Vinaigrette:
Combine all the
vinaigrette ingredients
in a frying pan and
warm over low heat.
2. Blanch the beans in
boiling water for
4–6 minutes. Add the
chicken to the
vinaigrette. Gently
warm through.
3. Drain the beans and

add to the pan with the
tomatoes. Remove
from the heat, stir in
the Gruyère cheese and
toss lightly.

NUTRITION PER SERVE
*Protein 45 g; Fat 50 g;
Carbohydrate 5 g; Dietary
Fibre 5 g; Cholesterol
160 mg; 2765 kJ (660 cal)*

Note: 'Topped and
tailed' means to trim
both stalk ends off each
bean. Use barbecued
chicken, leftover roast
chicken or breast fillets.

Herb Crumbed Chicken Pockets

*Ready to eat in
30 minutes
Serves 4*

*4 chicken breast fillets
4 teaspoons wholegrain
mustard
4 slices Swiss cheese
4 slices smoked ham
plain flour, for dusting
2 eggs, lightly beaten
1 cup (100 g/3 1/3 oz)
dried breadcrumbs
1 teaspoon grated
lemon rind
2 tablespoons chopped
fresh parsley
oil, for frying
lemon wedges, to serve*

1. Carefully slice
horizontally through
the centre of each fillet

without cutting
all the way through.
Open out the fillet and
spread one side with
1 teaspoon of mustard.
Top with 1 slice each of
cheese and ham,
making sure they do
not overlap the edge of
the fillet. Fold over the
fillet to enclose the
filling. Thread
2 toothpicks along the
cut edge. Repeat with
the remaining fillets.
2. Place the flour and
beaten eggs in two
separate shallow bowls.
Combine the
breadcrumbs, rind and
parsley on a flat plate.
Dip the fillets in the
flour, then the egg,
then the breadcrumb
mixture.
3. Heat enough oil in a
large, heavy-based pan
to come halfway up the
side of each fillet. Add
the fillets and cook for
8 minutes, turning
once, until cooked and
golden. Drain on paper
towels, remove the
toothpicks and serve
with lemon wedges.

NUTRITION PER SERVE
*Protein 55 g; Fat 20 g;
Carbohydrate 20 g; Dietary
Fibre 2 g; Cholesterol
200 mg; 1950 kJ (465 cal)*

Hint: Leave one end of
the toothpicks clearly
showing so that they
are easy to find and
remove after cooking.

*Green Bean and Chicken Salad (top) with
Herb Crumbed Chicken Pockets*

Hot and Spicy Chicken Wings

*Ready to eat in
30 minutes*
Serves 4

12 chicken wings,
  halved
2 tablespoons sesame
  oil
1–2 fresh chillies,
  seeded and chopped
2 tablespoons fennel
  seeds
2 tablespoons sesame
  seeds
1 tablespoon grated
  fresh ginger
3 cloves garlic, crushed
2 tablespoons soy sauce
1/4 cup (60 ml/2 fl oz)
  dry sherry
1/4 cup (90 g/3 oz)
  honey

1. Trim as much fat as possible from the chicken wings using a pair of kitchen scissors.
2. Heat the oil in a heavy-based pan and stir-fry the chicken wings for 5 minutes. Add the chilli, fennel, sesame seeds, ginger and garlic. Stir-fry for 30 seconds before adding the remaining ingredients. Cover and reduce the heat to low. Cook for 12–15 minutes, stirring occasionally, until all the syrup is absorbed.
3. Serve with cooked noodles or rice.

NUTRITION PER SERVE
*Protein 15 g; Fat 20 g;
Carbohydrate 20 g; Dietary
Fibre 2 g; Cholesterol
40 mg; 1315 kJ (315 cal)*

Moroccan Chicken

*Ready to eat in
30 minutes*
Serves 4–6

1 1/2 teaspoons cumin
1 teaspoon cinnamon
1 1/2 teaspoons paprika
1 teaspoon ground
  coriander
1/4 teaspoon ground
  cloves
1/4 teaspoon cayenne
  pepper (optional)
1 teaspoon ground
  ginger
1/4 teaspoon ground
  saffron
1 1/2 teaspoons sea
  salt
2 cloves garlic, crushed
2 tablespoons freshly
  squeezed lemon juice
1 tablespoon olive oil
850 g (1 lb 11 3/4 oz)
  chicken thigh fillets
2 tablespoons oil
1 cup (250 ml/8 fl oz)
  chicken stock
250 g (8 oz) instant
  couscous
40 g (1 1/3 oz) butter
grated rind of 1 lemon
1/4 cup (30 g/1 oz)
  sultanas
2 tablespoons slivered
  almonds

1. Place the cumin, cinnamon, paprika, coriander, cloves, cayenne (if using), ginger, saffron, salt, garlic, juice and oil in a bowl. Mix well, until a smooth paste is formed.
2. Brush the paste over the chicken fillets and set aside in a bowl for at least 5 minutes.
3. Heat the oil in a frying pan over moderate heat and cook the chicken thighs with any juices for 15–20 minutes, or until cooked through.
4. Meanwhile, bring the stock to the boil in a pan and add the couscous. Cover and remove from the heat. Set aside for 5 minutes, until the stock is absorbed, then fluff with a fork to separate the grains. Stir through the butter. Add the rind, sultanas and almonds; mix well. Spoon the couscous onto heated serving plates. Slice the chicken and arrange on top of the couscous. Spoon over any pan juices and serve immediately.

NUTRITION PER SERVE (6)
*Protein 35 g; Fat 20 g;
Carbohydrate 25 g; Dietary
Fibre 2 g; Cholesterol
115 mg; 1790 kJ (425 cal)*

*Hot and Spicy Chicken Wings (top)
with Moroccan Chicken*

Chicken and Mushrooms in Parchment

Preheat the oven to moderately hot 190°C (375°F/Gas 5). Finely chop 2 cloves garlic and a 4 cm (1¹/2 inch) piece of ginger. Chop 4 spring onions into matchsticks. Cut four 30 cm (12 inch) squares of baking paper and place a chicken breast fillet on each piece. Scatter the garlic, ginger and spring onion over each fillet. Top with 4 sliced shiitake mushrooms, 4 shredded kaffir lime leaves, a teaspoon of lime juice and a teaspoon of soy sauce. Season with salt and pepper. Fold in the sides of the paper to form a parcel. Lift onto an oven tray and bake for 20 minutes. Serve immediately with lime wedges.
Ready to eat in 30 minutes. Serves 4

NUTRITION PER SERVE
Protein 40 g; Fat 6 g; Carbohydrate 1 g; Dietary Fibre 1 g; Cholesterol 95 mg; 930 kJ (225 cal)

Piquant Chicken

Chop 6 chicken thigh fillets (about 500 g/ 1 lb) into bite-sized pieces; set aside. Heat 2 tablespoons olive oil in a large heavy-based frying pan. Add 2 chopped cloves garlic; cook for 30 seconds. Add the chopped chicken thigh fillets and cook, stirring often, over high heat for 5 minutes, or until the chicken begins to brown. Add 3 diced tomatoes, 1 teaspoon dried basil and

From left to right: Chicken and Mushrooms in Parchment; Piquant Chicken; Chicken, Potato and Spinach Curry

28

2 tablespoons each of small capers and balsamic vinegar. Bring the mixture to the boil; reduce the heat and simmer, uncovered, for 8 minutes. Stir in 2 teaspoons soft brown sugar and season with salt and freshly ground black pepper, to taste.
Ready to eat in 30 minutes. Serves 4

NUTRITION PER SERVE
Protein 25 g; Fat 15 g; Carbohydrate 5 g; Dietary Fibre 2 g; Cholesterol 85 mg; 1110 kJ (265 cal)

Chicken, Potato and Spinach Curry

Thaw 250 g (8 oz) of frozen chopped spinach. Heat 2 tablespoons oil in a heavy-based pan. Add 1 chopped onion, 2 tablespoons Indian curry paste and 1 large diced potato. Stir over moderate-high heat for 5 minutes, or until the potato begins to brown. Add 1 cup (250 ml/8 fl oz) chicken stock and bring to a rapid boil. Add 4 chopped chicken thigh fillets (about 350 g/11¼ oz) and the spinach. Reduce the heat and simmer, covered, for 7 minutes. Season with a pinch of salt and 2 tablespoons fresh lime juice. Serve.
Ready to eat in 30 minutes. Serves 4

NUTRITION PER SERVE
Protein 25 g; Fat 20 g; Carbohydrate 15 g; Dietary Fibre 5 g; Cholesterol 60 mg; 1305 kJ (310 cal)

Note: For a creamier curry, use coconut milk or cream instead of half the stock.

Gingered Chicken and Mushrooms

*Ready to eat in
30 minutes
Serves 4–6*

2 tablespoons cornflour
1 cup (250 ml/8 fl oz)
  chicken stock
2 tablespoons soy sauce
2 tablespoons freshly
  squeezed lemon juice
2 tablespoons
  sesame oil
4 chicken breast fillets,
  cut into thin strips
2 red capsicums, seeded
  and thinly sliced
2 tablespoons grated
  fresh ginger
$^1/2$ cup (50 g/1$^2/3$ oz)
  bamboo shoots, sliced
1$^1/2$ cups (150 g/5 oz)
  mixed mushrooms
  (shiitake, oyster, flat,
  Swiss brown, etc),
  halved
2 tablespoons chopped
  fresh basil

1. Dissolve the
cornflour in a quarter
of the stock. Add the
soy sauce, lemon juice
and remaining stock.
Set aside.
2. Heat the oil in a
wok. Add the chicken,
capsicum, ginger,
bamboo shoots and
mushrooms. Cook,
stirring, for
4–6 minutes, until the
chicken is cooked.
3. Stir in the liquid and
basil and bring to the
boil to thicken. Season
with salt and pepper, to
taste. Serve with
steamed rice.

NUTRITION PER SERVE (6)
*Protein 25 g; Fat 10 g;
Carbohydrate 10 g; Dietary
Fibre 1 g; Cholesterol
55 mg; 955 kJ (230 cal)*

Chicken Pawpaw Salad with Ginger Dressing

*Ready to eat in
30 minutes
Serves 4*

4 chicken breast fillets
1 tablespoon oil
1 tablespoon light soy
  sauce
1 teaspoon honey
1 red capsicum, seeded
2 small zucchini
1 celery stick
3 spring onions, sliced
$^1/3$ cup (20 g/$^2/3$ oz)
  chopped fresh
  coriander leaves
750 g (1$^1/2$ lb) pawpaw
$^1/2$ cup (80 g/2$^2/3$ oz)
  toasted unsalted
  macadamia nuts,
  roughly chopped

Ginger Dressing
1 tablespoon grated
  fresh ginger
3 tablespoons mirin
3 tablespoons oil, extra
1 tablespoon light soy
  sauce
2 teaspoons honey

1. Preheat the oven to
hot 210°C (415°F/
Gas 6–7). Place the
chicken in an
ovenproof dish and
coat with the combined
oil, soy sauce and
honey. Cover with foil
and bake for
15 minutes, until
tender. Cool, then slice
the fillets into thin
strips. Set aside.
2. Meanwhile, cut the
capsicum, zucchini and
celery into 5 cm
(2 inch) long, thin
strips. Place in a large
bowl with the onion
and coriander. Add the
chicken; mix well. Chop
the pawpaw into 2 cm
($^3/4$ inch) cubes; gently
stir into the salad.
3. **To make Ginger
Dressing:** Place the
ingredients in a jar and
shake well to combine.
Pour over the salad and
carefully fold through.
Scatter the macadamia
nuts on top and serve.

NUTRITION PER SERVE
*Protein 40 g; Fat 25 g;
Carbohydrate 20 g; Dietary
Fibre 5 g; Cholesterol
80 mg; 1890 kJ (450 cal)*

Note: Mirin is a low
alcohol sweet Japanese
cooking wine made
from rice.

*Gingered Chicken and Mushrooms (top) and
Chicken Pawpaw Salad with Ginger Dressing*

Greek Chicken Salad

Ready to eat in 30 minutes
Serves 4

1 barbecued chicken, boned, skinned and shredded
1 cucumber, cut into matchsticks
150 g (4³/4 oz) feta cheese, diced
1/3 cup (50 g/1²/3 oz) pine nuts, toasted
4 tomatoes, cut into wedges
3 spring onions, chopped
1/2 cup (60 g/2 oz) pitted black olives
2–3 cups (70 g/2¹/3 oz) mixed lettuce leaves

Dressing
2/3 cup (175 ml/5¹/2 fl oz) light olive oil
2 cloves garlic, crushed
3 tablespoons black olive paste

1. Place the chicken, cucumber, feta, pine nuts, tomato, spring onion and olives in a large bowl; mix well until combined.
2. **To make Dressing:** Combine all the dressing ingredients in a jar; shake well. Pour over the chicken mixture; toss lightly.
3. Line a bowl with lettuce leaves and spoon the chicken mixture on top.

NUTRITION PER SERVE
Protein 50 g; Fat 70 g; Carbohydrate 7 g; Dietary Fibre 5 g; Cholesterol 190 mg; 3530 kJ (845 cal)

Sweet Soy Chicken with Bok Choy

Ready to eat in 30 minutes
Serves 4

4 bok choy
1 tablespoon oil
4 teaspoons sesame oil
2 chicken breast fillets, cut into thick strips
2 small fresh red chillies, seeded and finely chopped
2 teaspoons grated fresh ginger
6 spring onions, sliced
1 small red capsicum, thinly sliced
450 g (14¹/3 oz) Hokkien noodles
1/2 cup (25 g/³/4 oz) chopped fresh coriander
2 tablespoons kecap manis (see note)

1. Soak the bok choy in a basin of cold water for 2–3 minutes; drain. Separate the leaves and set aside.
2. Heat the oil with 1 teaspoon of the sesame oil in a large wok. Add the chicken and stir-fry over high heat for 3–4 minutes, until cooked. Set aside.
3. Heat 2 teaspoons of the sesame oil in the wok. Add the chilli, ginger, spring onion and capsicum. Stir-fry over high heat for 2–3 minutes, or until softened. Set aside.
4. Heat the remaining sesame oil in the wok, then add the bok choy. Stir-fry for 1 minute. Set aside, keeping warm. Meanwhile, place the noodles in a large bowl, cover with boiling water and set aside.
5. Return the chicken, bok choy and vegetables to the wok and heat through. Add the coriander and kecap manis; stir-fry for 2–3 minutes more.
6. Drain the noodles and top with the chicken mixture.

NUTRITION PER SERVE
Protein 30 g; Fat 15 g; Carbohydrate 50 g; Dietary Fibre 1 g; Cholesterol 40 mg; 1880 kJ (450 cal)

Note: Kecap manis is a very sweet, thick soy sauce. Hokkien noodles are always sold ready to use, being pre-cooked and lightly oiled.

Greek Chicken Salad (top) with Sweet Soy Chicken with Bok Choy

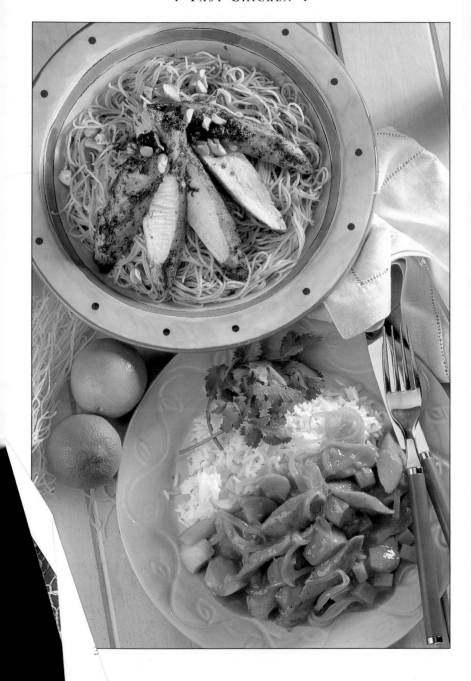

Spicy Coriander Chicken

*Ready to eat in
30 minutes
Serves 4*

*1 bunch (90 g/3 oz)
fresh coriander,
including the roots
2–3 cloves garlic
2–3 small fresh red
chillies
1 tablespoon caster
sugar
2 teaspoons grated lime
rind
3 tablespoons lime juice
2 tablespoons kecap
manis (see note)
1 tablespoon oil, plus
2 teaspoons, extra
4 chicken breast fillets
250 g (8 oz) rice stick
noodles
chopped fresh
coriander leaves,
extra, to garnish
1/2 cup (80 g/2 2/3 oz)
unsalted cashews,
toasted, chopped*

1. Wash the coriander and shake to remove excess water. Roughly chop the garlic and chillies in a food processor or blender, then add the coriander. Process for a further 15 seconds. Add the sugar, lime rind and lime juice, kecap manis and 1 tablespoon of the oil. Process until smooth.
2. Lightly slash the chicken fillets. Place in a bowl and coat with about one-quarter of the coriander mixture; set aside for 5 minutes.
3. Heat a heavy-based pan with the extra oil. Cook the chicken fillets for 3–4 minutes each side, turning once, until cooked through. Brush 2–3 times with the marinade while cooking. Cut each fillet into strips.
4. Meanwhile, cook the noodles in a large pan of boiling water for 5 minutes, until tender. Drain, and pour over most of the remaining coriander mixture. Toss to combine. Divide the noodles among 4 serving plates and top with the sliced chicken breast and a spoonful of the remaining coriander mixture. Garnish with chopped coriander and cashews. Serve with a green salad, if desired.

NUTRITION PER SERVE
*Protein 40 g; Fat 20 g;
Carbohydrate 25 g; Dietary
Fibre 2 g; Cholesterol
80 mg; 1890 kJ (450 cal)*

Note: Kecap manis is a sweet soy sauce.

*Spicy Coriander Chicken (top)
with Curried Chicken Sausages*

Curried Chicken Sausages

*Ready to eat in
30 minutes
Serves 4*

*10 chicken sausages
1 1/2 tablespoons oil
3 onions, sliced
2 cloves garlic, crushed
1–2 teaspoons curry
powder
1 teaspoon paprika
1 teaspoon turmeric
1 cup (250 ml/8 fl oz)
chicken stock
1/2 cup (125 ml/4 fl oz)
apple juice
2 green apples, cored
and roughly chopped
1 sweet potato, finely
diced*

1. Prick the sausages and boil for 6 minutes. Drain and thinly slice.
2. Heat the oil in a large, heavy-based pan; cook the onion and garlic until soft. Add the curry powder, paprika and turmeric. Stir for 30 seconds before adding the stock, sausage, apple juice, apples and sweet potato. Season with salt and pepper, to taste. Simmer, uncovered, for 10 minutes over low heat. Serve with rice.

NUTRITION PER SERVE
*Protein 40 g; Fat 45 g;
Carbohydrate 45 g; Dietary
Fibre 10 g; Cholesterol
135 mg; 3035 kJ (725 cal)*

Parmesan Chicken with Garlic Butter

Cut 4 chicken breast fillets into thick strips. Dust with flour, shaking off any excess. Whisk together 2 eggs. In a separate bowl, combine 2 cups (160 g/5^1/4 oz) fresh breadcrumbs with ^{1}/2 cup (50 g/1^2/3 oz) grated fresh Parmesan cheese. Dip the chicken pieces, one at a time, into the egg, then roll in the breadcrumb mixture to coat. Heat a little oil in a frying pan. Cook the chicken in batches over moderate heat for 1–2 minutes each side, until cooked through. Drain on paper towels and keep warm. Melt 50 g (1^2/3 oz) butter in a pan. Add 4 crushed cloves garlic and cook for 2–3 minutes. Add 2 tablespoons chopped fresh parsley; season to taste with salt and pepper. Pour over the warm chicken.
Ready to eat in 20 minutes. Serves 4

NUTRITION PER SERVE
Protein 40 g; Fat 20 g; Carbohydrate 30 g; Dietary Fibre 2 g; Cholesterol 190 mg; 1960 kJ (470 cal)

Chicken with Capsicum and Chilli Sauce

Cut 2 red capsicums into thin strips. Heat 2 tablespoons olive oil in a heavy-based pan. Add 1 teaspoon dried chilli flakes and the capsicum; cook over low heat for 10 minutes. Meanwhile, heat a little oil in a separate pan. Add 4 chicken breast fillets and cook for 2–3 minutes each side, until well browned.

Reduce the heat and add 2 tablespoons dry white wine. Simmer, covered, for 5 minutes. Stir 1/2 cup (125 ml/ 4 fl oz) cream into the braised capsicum and season with salt and pepper. Spoon the capsicum sauce over the chicken fillets, and sprinkle with fresh oregano leaves to serve.
Ready to eat in 30 minutes. Serves 4

NUTRITION PER SERVE
Protein 30 g; Fat 30 g; Carbohydrate 5 g; Dietary Fibre 1 g; Cholesterol 100 mg; 1720 kJ (410 cal)

Thai Chicken Sauté

Cut 4 chicken breast fillets into thick strips. Combine with 2 tablespoons green curry paste and 1 tablespoon oil in a bowl. Mix well and set aside for 10 minutes. Heat a heavy-based frying pan with a little oil. Cook the chicken in a single layer for about 2 minutes each side. Drizzle over 1/3 cup (80 ml/2 3/4 fl oz) coconut milk and 2 tablespoons lime juice. Turn the chicken pieces in the sauce before serving. Garnish with fresh coriander leaves for an authentic Thai flavour.
Ready to eat in 30 minutes. Serves 4

NUTRITION PER SERVE
Protein 35 g; Fat 15 g; Carbohydrate 5 g; Dietary Fibre 0 g; Cholesterol 75 mg; 1280 kJ (305 cal)

Note: Good quality commercial curry pastes are available from Asian food stores, delicatessens and supermarkets.

From left to right: Parmesan Chicken with Garlic Butter; Chicken with Capsicum and Chilli Sauce; Thai Chicken Sauté

Chicken and Corn Soup

*Ready to eat in
  30 minutes
Serves 6–8*

6 cups (1.5 litres)
  chicken stock
440 g (14 oz) can corn
  kernels, drained
420 g (13^1/3 oz) can
  creamed corn
8 spring onions, finely
  chopped
1 tablespoon grated
  fresh ginger
1 tablespoon cornflour
2 egg whites
1 tablespoon soy sauce
2 cups (350 g/11^1/4 oz)
  shredded barbecued
  chicken

1. Combine the chicken stock, drained corn kernels, creamed corn, three-quarters of the finely chopped spring onions and the grated fresh ginger in a large, heavy-based pan. Slowly bring to the boil while stirring. Boil for 2 minutes.
2. Add the cornflour to 1 tablespoon water in a small bowl and mix to a smooth paste. Gradually add to the soup, stirring, until the soup boils and thickens. Simmer for 1–2 minutes.
3. Whisk together the egg whites and 2 tablespoons water in a small jug. Slowly add to the soup in a thin stream, stirring constantly to combine. Do not allow the mixture to boil.
4. Add the soy sauce and shredded chicken. Stir to combine and simmer for 2–3 minutes, until the chicken is heated through. Garnish with the remaining chopped spring onion and serve.

NUTRITION PER SERVE (8)
*Protein 15 g; Fat 5 g;
Carbohydrate 25 g; Dietary
Fibre 5 g; Cholesterol
55 mg; 829 kJ (200 cal)*

Mixed Grill

*Ready to eat in
  30 minutes
Serves 4*

Dipping Sauce
1 cup (250 g/8 oz)
  chilled mayonnaise
2 cloves garlic, crushed
1 teaspoon lemon juice
2 teaspoons chopped
  fresh basil

^{3}/4 cup (80 ml/
  2^3/4 fl oz) ready-made
  herb and garlic salad
  dressing
4 chicken breast or
  thigh fillets, halved
2 slender eggplants,
  sliced lengthways
4 zucchini, halved
2 red capsicums, cut in
  thick strips
4 field mushrooms,
  halved
2 egg tomatoes, halved

1. To make Dipping Sauce: Combine the mayonnaise, crushed garlic, lemon juice and chopped basil in a small bowl. Chill until ready to use.
2. Preheat the grill. Brush the chicken, eggplant, zucchini, capsicum, mushrooms and tomatoes with the herb and garlic dressing. Place the chicken and all the vegetables except the tomatoes on the grill pan.
3. Once the vegetables are starting to soften, add the tomatoes. When the chicken and vegetables are cooked through and golden on all sides, remove from the heat. Serve immediately with the Dipping Sauce.

NUTRITION PER SERVE
*Protein 50 g; Fat 30 g;
Carbohydrate 50 g; Dietary
Fibre 10 g; Cholesterol
100 mg; 2740 kJ (655 cal)*

Note: Herb and garlic salad dressing can be found in most good supermarkets.

---

*Chicken and Corn Soup (top)
with Mixed Grill*

Tandoori Chicken Pizza

Ready to eat in 30 minutes
Serves 4

Cucumber Yoghurt Topping
200 g (6 1/2 oz) plain yoghurt
1 Lebanese cucumber, grated
1 tablespoon chopped fresh mint

8 chicken tenderloins, sliced
1 tablespoon tandoori paste
2 tablespoons plain yoghurt
1 tablespoon oil
3 tablespoons mango chutney
1 ready-made pizza base (diameter 28 cm/ 11 inches)
1/4 cup (35 g/1 1/4 oz) grated mozzarella
1 small red onion, sliced into rings
fresh mint leaves, to garnish

1. Preheat the oven to moderately hot 200°C (400°F/Gas 6).
2. To make Cucumber Yoghurt Topping: Combine all the topping ingredients and set aside.
3. Combine the chicken, tandoori paste and yoghurt. Heat the oil in a frying pan. Add the chicken pieces and fry over medium-high heat for 3–4 minutes.
4. Spread the mango chutney over the pizza base. Top with the mozzarella and onion. Scatter the chicken over the top. Bake in the oven for 10 minutes. Serve warm with the Cucumber Yoghurt Dressing. Garnish with the mint leaves.

NUTRITION PER SERVE
Protein 35 g; Fat 25 g; Carbohydrate 15 g; Dietary Fibre 1 g; Cholesterol 95 mg; 1655 kJ (395 cal)

Mediterranean Chicken Salad

Ready to eat in 30 minutes
Serves 6–8

1 barbecued chicken, shredded
400 g (12 2/3 oz) can artichoke hearts, drained and quartered
6 egg tomatoes, quartered
1 small fennel bulb, sliced
1 small red onion, sliced into thin rings
1 Lebanese cucumber, peeled and sliced
12 Kalamata olives
125 g (4 oz) feta cheese, cubed
3 hard-boiled eggs, peeled and quartered
1/3 cup (20 g/2/3 oz) chopped fresh basil

Garlic Dressing
1/2 cup (125 ml/4 fl oz) olive oil
2 tablespoons white wine vinegar
1–2 cloves garlic, crushed
1 teaspoon Dijon mustard
1/2 teaspoon dried oregano
1/2 teaspoon caster sugar

1. Place the chicken, artichoke, tomato, fennel, onion, cucumber and olives in a large bowl and toss to combine.
2. To make Garlic Dressing: Shake all the dressing ingredients in a jar to combine. Pour the dressing over the chicken mixture and mix well.
3. Add the feta, eggs and basil to the bowl. Gently mix in so as not to break up the eggs and feta. If preferred, arrange the eggs on top of the salad.

NUTRITION PER SERVE (8)
Protein 25 g; Fat 25 g; Carbohydrate 5 g; Dietary Fibre 5 g; Cholesterol 170 mg; 1500 kJ (360 cal)

Tandoori Chicken Pizza (top) with Mediterranean Chicken Salad

Chicken Sesame Goujons with Aïoli

Cut 4 chicken breast fillets into thick strips. Place some flour on a plate with a little salt and pepper. Dust the chicken in the seasoned flour. Whisk together 2 eggs and then dip the chicken strips in the egg, one piece at a time. Combine $1^2/3$ cup (135 g/$4^1/2$ oz) fresh breadcrumbs with 2 tablespoons sesame seeds; roll the chicken in the mixture. Heat a large frying pan with 2 tablespoons oil and 30 g (1 oz) butter. Add the chicken in batches and cook for 2–3 minutes each side, until cooked through. Meanwhile, make the Aïoli by combining $1/2$ cup (125 g/4 oz) whole egg mayonnaise, 2 tablespoons finely chopped fresh parsley and 1–2 crushed cloves garlic. Serve the chicken with Aïoli and salad.
Ready to eat in 30 minutes. Serves 4

NUTRITION PER SERVE
Protein 45 g; Fat 40 g; Carbohydrate 30 g; Dietary Fibre 5 g; Cholesterol 250 mg; 2785 kJ (665 cal)

German-style Chicken with Sautéed Apple

Peel and core 2 green apples; cut into small wedges. Cut 3 chicken breast fillets (about 400 g/$12^2/3$ oz) into long thin strips. Heat 2 tablespoons oil in a heavy-based frying pan. Fry the chicken over high heat for 4 minutes, until golden; set aside. Heat 30 g (1 oz) butter in the pan. Add the apple and 2 teaspoons soft brown sugar. Cook, stirring, for 5 minutes, until the

apples are a light golden colour. Add 2 tablespoons brandy; stir until evaporated. Stir in 300 ml (9 1/2 fl oz) cream and 2 teaspoons wholegrain mustard. Return the chicken to the pan. Bring the sauce to the boil; reduce the heat and simmer for 3 minutes. Season well with salt and pepper. *Ready to eat in 30 minutes. Serves 4*

NUTRITION PER SERVE
Protein 35 g; Fat 65 g; Carbohydrate 15 g; Dietary Fibre 2 g; Cholesterol 230 mg; 3425 kJ (820 cal)

Citrus Chicken With Oregano

Preheat the oven to moderate 180°C (350°F/Gas 4). Place 500 g (1 lb) chicken tenderloins in a large baking dish. Combine 1/4 cup (60 ml/2 fl oz) olive oil, 1/3 cup (80 ml/2 3/4 fl oz) lemon juice, 2 tablespoons chopped fresh oregano in a jug, and season to taste with salt and freshly ground black pepper. Pour the mixture over the tenderloins and turn the pieces to coat thoroughly. Bake for 15–20 minutes, or until the tenderloins are tender and cooked through. Serve with couscous or rice. *Ready to eat in 30 minutes. Serves 4*

NUTRITION PER SERVE
Protein 25 g; Fat 20 g; Carbohydrate 0 g; Dietary Fibre 0 g; Cholesterol 85 mg; 1180 kJ (280 cal)

From left to right: Chicken Sesame Goujons with Aïoli; German-style Chicken and Apple Simmer; Citrus Chicken with Oregano

Ginger Chicken Salad

*Ready to eat in
30 minutes*
Serves 4

4 chicken breast fillets
2 teaspoons oil
1 red capsicum
1 green capsicum
2 yellow zucchini
*6 spring onions, thinly
    sliced*
*1/3 cup (20 g/2/3 oz)
    chopped fresh
    coriander*
*1/2 cup (80 g/2 2/3 oz)
    toasted cashews,
    roughly chopped*
*mixed salad leaves for
    serving*

Ginger Dressing
4 tablespoons oil
*1 1/2 tablespoons rice
    wine vinegar*
1 tablespoon honey
*1 tablespoon grated
    fresh ginger*
*2 teaspoons light soy
    sauce*

1. Preheat the oven to
hot 210°C (415°F/
Gas 6–7). Place the
chicken fillets in an
ovenproof dish in a
single layer, and lightly
brush with oil. Cover
loosely with foil and
bake for 15 minutes, or
until just cooked. Set
aside to cool slightly.
2. Meanwhile, cut the
capsicums into strips,
slice the zucchini
diagonally and put in a
bowl with the spring
onion and coriander.
Mix together.
**3. To make Ginger
Dressing:** Place all the
dressing ingredients in
a jar; shake to combine.
4. Slice the chicken
fillets into 5 cm (2 inch)
diagonal strips and add
to the vegetables. Pour
the dressing over the
salad, coating the
chicken and vegetables
well. Serve on a layer of
salad leaves and
sprinkle with cashews.

NUTRITION PER SERVE
*Protein 40 g; Fat 35 g;
Carbohydrate 15 g; Dietary
Fibre 5 g; Cholesterol
80 mg; 2260 kJ (540 cal)*

Pâté-stuffed Chicken Breast

*Ready to eat in
30 minutes*
Serves 4

*4 chicken breast fillets
    (with skin left on)*
*4 tablespoons chicken
    liver pâté*
60 g (2 oz) butter
*1/2 cup (125 ml/4 fl oz)
    cream*
1 teaspoon cornflour
*1/4 cup (60 ml/2 fl oz)
    freshly squeezed
    lemon juice*
*2 tablespoons chopped
    fresh parsley*

1. Lift up the skin of
the chicken (keeping it
attached to the breast)
and slip 1 tablespoon
of pâté between the
skin and the flesh of
each breast. Secure
with skewers.
2. Heat the butter in a
pan and cook both
sides of the chicken
until brown. Cover and
cook over moderate
heat for 12 minutes,
until the chicken is
cooked. Transfer to a
hot dish. Cover and
keep warm.
3. Pour almost all the
cream into the pan with
the remaining juices
and brush down the
side of the pan. Mix the
cornflour with the
lemon juice and the
remaining cream in a
cup. Stir until smooth,
add to the pan and stir
well. Add the parsley
and season with salt
and black pepper. Stir
until the sauce boils
and thickens. Spoon
over the chicken and
serve with vegetables.

NUTRITION PER SERVE
*Protein 40 g; Fat 35 g;
Carbohydrate 2 g; Dietary
Fibre 0 g; Cholesterol
195 mg; 2000 kJ (480 cal))*

Hint: Try using a
Grand Marnier or
peppercorn pâté.

*Ginger Chicken Salad (top) with
Pâté-stuffed Chicken Breast*

Chicken with Couscous Tabbouleh

Ready to eat in 30 minutes
Serves 4

4 chicken breast fillets
2 tablespoons olive oil
1 tablespoon lemon juice
1 teaspoon dried oregano
300 g (10 oz) hummus

Couscous Tabbouleh
250 g (8 oz) instant couscous
1 cup (250 ml/8 fl oz) hot chicken stock
1/3 cup (80 ml/ 2 3/4 fl oz) lemon juice
2 tablespoons olive oil
4 spring onions, finely chopped
8 cherry tomatoes, quartered
1 cup (30 g/1oz) finely chopped fresh parsley
1/2 cup (25 g/3/4 oz) finely chopped fresh coriander

1. Slash the chicken fillets. Place in a dish and pour over the combined oil, juice and oregano. Set aside.
2. **To make Couscous Tabbouleh:** Place the couscous in a large bowl with the hot stock. Stir, then cover and set aside. Combine the juice and oil in a jar. Season with salt and pepper; set aside.
3. Heat a heavy-based pan. Add the chicken; cook for 2 minutes each side. Reduce the heat to moderate and cook for 3–4 minutes each side, until cooked through. Brush often with the marinade.
4. Add the spring onion, tomato, parsley and coriander to the couscous. Stir through the dressing. Slice the chicken and serve on top of the couscous with the hummus.

NUTRITION PER SERVE
Protein 50 g; Fat 35 g; Carbohydrate 40 g; Dietary Fibre 10 g; Cholesterol 80 mg; 2810 kJ (670 cal)

Turkish Sandwiches

Ready to eat in 30 minutes
Serves 4

2 tablespoons olive oil
2 cloves garlic, crushed
1/2 teaspoon dried oregano
pide bread, cut into 4 pieces
4 slender eggplant
12 chicken tenderloins
2 tablespoons pesto sauce
1/2 cup (125 g/4 oz) whole egg mayonnaise
4 large pieces sun-dried capsicum, drained
2 large tomatoes, sliced
Haloumi cheese, sliced

1. Preheat the grill. Combine the oil, garlic and oregano. Cut the pide bread pieces in half lengthways; brush with the oil mixture. Grill both sides until browned.
2. Cut the eggplant into quarters lengthways (leave the end attached). Brush with the oil mixture. Fan out and grill for 3–4 minutes, turning, until cooked. Set aside.
3. Brush the chicken with the oil mixture. Grill for 3–4 minutes, turning, until cooked.
4. Combine the pesto and mayonnaise.
5. Place one eggplant, a piece of sun-dried capsicum and 3 chicken tenderloins on each bread base. Top each with 2–3 tomato slices and a couple of slices of cheese. Place under the grill with the tops alongside for 1–2 minutes to warm and melt the cheese. Serve with pesto mayonnaise.

NUTRITION PER SERVE
Protein 35 g; Fat 35 g; Carbohydrate 55 g; Dietary Fibre 10 g; Cholesterol 95 mg; 2830 kJ (675 cal)

Chicken with Couscous Tabbouleh (top) with Turkish Sandwiches

Poached Chicken with Salsa Verde

*Ready to eat in
30 minutes
Serves 6*

6 chicken breast fillets
1 cup (250 ml/8 fl oz)
 white wine
1 teaspoon grated
 lemon rind
1 tablespoon freshly
 squeezed lemon juice
a few whole peppercorns
mixed salad leaves, to
 serve

Salsa Verde
1 cup (50 g/1²/3 oz)
 fresh basil leaves
1 cup (50 g/1²/3 oz)
 fresh mint leaves
2 tablespoons capers
1 tablespoon caster
 sugar
1 teaspoon grated
 lemon rind
1 tablespoon freshly
 squeezed lemon juice
2 cloves garlic, crushed
1 slice white bread
3 anchovy fillets,
 drained (optional)
¹/3 cup (80 ml/
 2³/4 fl oz) olive oil

1. Preheat the oven to
moderate 180°C
(350°F/Gas 4). Place
the chicken in an
ovenproof dish. Pour
over the combined
wine, rind, juice and
peppercorns. Cook for
20 minutes, turning
once, until just tender.

Slice, then place on the
salad leaves.
2. **To make Salsa Verde:**
Place all the ingredients,
except the oil, in a food
processor and process
until smooth. With
the motor running,
slowly add the oil.
Serve with the chicken.

NUTRITION PER SERVE
*Protein 35 g; Fat 15 g;
Carbohydrate 5 g; Dietary
Fibre 1 g; Cholesterol
70 mg; 1380 kJ (330 cal)*

Fettucine with Chicken Mushroom Sauce

*Ready to eat in
30 minutes
Serves 4–6*

10 g (¹/3 oz) Porcini
 mushrooms
2 tablespoons olive oil
2 cloves garlic, crushed
200 g (6¹/2 oz) button
 mushrooms, sliced
125 g (4 oz) prosciutto,
 chopped
375 g (12 oz) fettucine
¹/4 cup (60 ml/2 fl oz)
 brandy
1 cup (250 ml/8 fl oz)
 cream
1 barbecued chicken,
 shredded
1 cup (155 g/5 oz)
 frozen peas
¹/3 cup (20 g/²/3 oz)
 chopped fresh parsley

1. Place the Porcini
mushrooms in a bowl
and cover with boiling
water. Set aside for
10 minutes, then drain,
squeeze dry and chop.
2. Heat the oil in a
large, heavy-based pan.
Add the garlic; cook,
stirring, for 1 minute
over low heat. Add the
button and porcini
mushrooms and
prosciutto and cook
over low heat, stirring
often, for 5 minutes.
3. Meanwhile, cook the
pasta in a large pan of
boiling water until
tender; drain.
4. Add the brandy and
cream to the mushroom
mixture. Cook, stirring,
over low heat for
2 minutes. Add the
chicken, peas and
parsley. Cook, stirring,
for 4–5 minutes, until
heated through. Add
the chicken mixture to
the hot pasta; mix well.
Serve with grated fresh
Parmesan, if desired.

NUTRITION PER SERVE (6)
*Protein 40 g; Fat 35 g;
Carbohydrate 45 g; Dietary
Fibre 5 g; Cholesterol
175 mg; 2775 kJ (660 cal)*

Note: If porcini
mushrooms are not
available, use
30 g (1 oz) dried
Chinese mushrooms.

*Poached Chicken with Salsa Verde (top) and
Fettucine with Chicken Mushroom Sauce*

Tandoori Chicken Skewers

Cut 4 chicken breast or thigh fillets into small pieces. Combine 250 g (8 oz) plain yoghurt, 2–3 crushed cloves garlic, 2 teaspoons each of ground turmeric and cumin, 1 teaspoon ground coriander and 1/2 teaspoon cayenne pepper in a bowl. Cut 1 onion into thin wedges. Thread the chicken pieces alternately with the onion onto wooden or metal skewers. Lay the skewers on a greased, foil-lined grill tray. Brush liberally with the yoghurt marinade and cook under a preheated grill for 8 minutes, or until cooked through. Turn the skewers often and brush with marinade while cooking.
Ready to eat in 30 minutes. Serves 4

NUTRITION PER SERVE
Protein 40 g; Fat 5 g; Carbohydrate 5 g; Dietary Fibre 1 g; Cholesterol 90 mg; 970 kJ (230 cal)

Chicken in a Light Creamy Blue Sauce

Cut 4 chicken breast fillets into thick strips. Melt 50 g (1 2/3 oz) butter in a heavy-based pan. Add the chicken and cook for 5 minutes, stirring regularly. Move the chicken to one side and add 3/4 cup (185 ml/6 fl oz) cream, 1/2 cup (125 ml/4 fl oz) chicken stock and 100 g (3 1/3 oz) crumbled blue-vein cheese. Stir until the cheese has melted.

From left to right: Tandoori Chicken Skewers; Chicken in a Light Creamy Blue Sauce; Chicken Tenderloins with a Trio of Herbs

Bring to the boil; reduce the heat and simmer for 7 minutes, or until the chicken is tender, turning occasionally. Season with salt and pepper. (Test the sauce first as you may find that it is salty enough already.) Stir in 2 tablespoons chopped fresh parsley. Serve with pasta.
Ready to eat in 30 minutes. Serves 4

NUTRITION PER SERVE
Protein 30 g; Fat 40 g; Carbohydrate 2 g; Dietary Fibre 0 g; Cholesterol 175 mg; 2070 kJ (495 cal)

Chicken Tenderloins with a Trio of Herbs

Place 500 g (1 lb) chicken tenderloins and 2 tablespoons of olive oil in a bowl with plenty of salt and freshly ground black pepper. Heat a cast iron grill plate or frying pan until very hot. Cook the chicken quickly in batches for 1^{1}/$_{2}$–2 minutes, turning each piece over as it browns. Transfer each batch to a bowl and keep warm. Add 3 tablespoons chopped fresh parsley, 2 teaspoons each of chopped fresh lemon thyme and oregano and 2 tablespoons lemon juice to the chicken. Toss together and serve immediately.
Ready to eat in 30 minutes. Serves 4

NUTRITION PER SERVE
Protein 25 g; Fat 15 g; Carbohydrate 0 g; Dietary Fibre 0 g; Cholesterol 85 mg; 1000 kJ (240 cal)

Sautéed Mushroom and Chicken Livers
*Ready to eat in
  25 minutes
Serves 4*

400 g (12²/3 oz)
  chicken livers
plain flour, to dust
1 tablespoon oil
50 g (1²/3 oz) butter
1 onion, sliced
2 teaspoons fresh
  thyme (or 1 teaspoon
  dried)
1 cup (90 g/3 oz)
  mushrooms, chopped

1. Rinse the livers and
remove any membrane.
Toss lightly in a dish of
flour. Heat the oil and
butter in a heavy-based
pan. Fry the livers until
cooked and brown,
then remove from the
pan and set aside.
2. Add the onion and
thyme to the pan and
cook until soft. Stir in
the mushrooms and
cook for 2 minutes,
then return the livers
to the pan. Cook until
heated through and
season with salt and
pepper, to taste.
3. Serve the mushroom
and livers piled up on a
dish of couscous.

NUTRITION PER SERVE
*Protein 20 g; Fat 20 g;
Carbohydrate 5 g; Dietary
Fibre 1 g; Cholesterol
450 mg; 1105 kJ (265 cal)*

Chicken Rolls with Mango Capsicum Salsa
*Ready to eat in
  30 minutes
Serves 6*

6 chicken breast fillets
2 tablespoons freshly
  squeezed orange juice
2 tablespoons lime juice
1 tablespoon chopped
  fresh coriander
1/2 teaspoon chilli
  powder
1/4 teaspoon cayenne
  pepper
1 teaspoon caster sugar
1 tablespoon oil, plus
  2 teaspoons oil
6 large Lebanese breads
1/2 cup (125 g/4 oz)
  light sour cream
cos lettuce leaves,
  to serve

Mango Capsicum Salsa
2 mangoes, diced
1 red capsicum, finely
  chopped
4 spring onions, finely
  chopped
1 small fresh red chilli,
  chopped (optional)
1/2 cup (25 g/3/4 oz)
  chopped fresh
  coriander
1 teaspoon grated lime
  rind
1 tablespoon lime juice

1. Slash the chicken
fillets. Combine the

orange and lime juices,
coriander, chilli
powder, cayenne, sugar
and 1 tablespoon of
the oil in a large dish.
Place the chicken in
the dish and coat
thoroughly with the
marinade. Set aside.
**2. To make Mango
Capsicum Salsa:**
Combine all the salsa
ingredients in a large
bowl. Set aside.
3. Heat a heavy-based
pan with the remaining
oil. Add the chicken
and cook for 3–4
minutes each side,
turning once, until
cooked through. Brush
with the marinade
while cooking. Cut
each fillet into strips
lengthways.
4. Coat one side of the
Lebanese bread with a
tablespoon of sour
cream. Lay a few
lettuce leaves on top,
then add the strips of
one chicken breast and
1/4 cup salsa. Roll the
bread up firmly and
repeat with the
remaining breads. Serve
with the remaining sour
cream and Mango
Capsicum Salsa.

NUTRITION PER SERVE
*Protein 45 g; Fat 15 g;
Carbohydrate 75 g; Dietary
Fibre 5 g; Cholesterol
85 mg; 2600 kJ (620 cal)*

*Sautéed Mushroom and Chicken Livers (top) with
Chicken Rolls with Mango Capsicum Salsa*

Chicken Stroganoff

*Ready to eat in
30 minutes*
Serves 4–6

4 *chicken breast fillets*
1 *tablespoon oil*
1 *onion, sliced*
200 g (6 1/2 oz) *button
mushrooms, halved*
3 *teaspoons sweet
paprika*
1 *tablespoon tomato
paste*
2 *teaspoons Dijon
mustard*
1/2 *cup (125 ml/4 fl oz)
white wine*
1/3 *cup (80 ml/
2 3/4 fl oz) chicken
stock*
1/2 *cup (125 g/4 oz)
sour cream*
2 *tablespoons chopped
fresh parsley*

1. Slice the chicken
breast fillets into strips.
Heat the oil in a large
heavy-based frying pan.
Cook the chicken over
medium-high heat for
4–5 minutes until
browned and cooked.
Remove and set aside.
2. Add the onion to the
pan and cook for
1–2 minutes. Stir in the
mushrooms and sweet
paprika. Cook for a
further 1 minute. Stir in
the combined tomato
paste, mustard, wine
and the chicken stock.
Bring to the boil,
reduce the heat and
simmer for 5 minutes.
3. Stir in the sour
cream and the chicken
strips. Heat through.
Season well with salt
and pepper. Garnish
with the chopped
parsley to serve.

NUTRITION PER SERVE
*Protein 25 g; Fat 15 g;
Carbohydrate 3 g; Dietary
Fibre 1.5 g; Cholesterol
80 mg; 1080 kJ (260 cal)*

Herbed Chicken Breast

*Ready to eat in
30 minutes*
Serves 4

150 g (5 oz) *ricotta*
2 *tablespoons grated
Parmesan*
1 *tablespoon chopped
fresh chives*
1 *tablespoon chopped
fresh parsley*
1 *tablespoon chopped
fresh basil*
4 *chicken breast fillets,
with skin left on*
1/4 *cup (60 ml/2 fl oz)
chicken stock*

Basil Dressing
2 *tablespoons extra
virgin olive oil*
2 *tablespoons tarragon
vinegar*
1 *clove garlic, crushed*
1/2 *teaspoon sugar*
1 *tablespoon shredded
fresh basil*

1. Preheat oven to hot
210°C (415°F/
Gas 6–7).Combine the
ricotta, grated
Parmesan, chopped
chives, parsley and
basil in a bowl. Season
well with salt
and pepper.
2. Divide the ricotta
mixture into
4 portions. Lift up the
skin of each chicken
breast (keeping it
attached) and slip a
portion of the ricotta
between the skin and
flesh. Secure with
toothpicks. Place in a
single layer in a baking
dish. Pour the stock
over the chicken fillets.
Bake for 20 minutes or
until brown. Remove
the toothpicks from the
chicken and set aside.
**3. To make Basil
Dressing:** Combine all
the ingredients in a jar
with 1 tablespoon of
the pan juices. Season
with salt and pepper
and shake to combine
well. Pour the dressing
over the chicken and
serve with sliced
tomatoes and fennel.

NUTRITION PER SERVE
*Protein 35 g; Fat 40 g;
Carbohydrate 4 g; Dietary
Fibre 1.5 g; Cholesterol
145 mg; 2135 kJ (510 cal)*

*Chicken Stroganoff (top)
with Herbed Chicken Breast*

Roasted Chicken and Tomatoes with Rosemary

Preheat the oven to moderate 180°C (350°F/Gas 4). Cut 6 egg tomatoes in half lengthways; place in a baking dish. Add 1 tablespoon chopped fresh rosemary, 8 unpeeled cloves garlic, 1/4 cup (60 ml/ 2 fl oz) each of olive oil and balsamic vinegar, 2 tablespoons white wine vinegar and some freshly ground black pepper. Top 4 chicken breast fillets with a sprig of fresh rosemary. Wrap a long piece of

prosciutto around, and secure the end with a toothpick. Add to the baking dish, rosemary-side up. Bake for 20 minutes. Remove the toothpicks. Serve with the tomatoes, pan juices and the garlic flesh. Sprinkle with cracked black pepper. Serve with potatoes and shavings of fresh Parmesan.
Ready to eat in 30 minutes. Serves 4

NUTRITION PER SERVE
Protein 45 g; Fat 25 g; Carbohydrate 2 g; Dietary Fibre 2 g; Cholesterol 100 mg; 1640 kJ (390 cal)

Asparagus Chicken

Cut 4 chicken breast fillets into thirds. Cover the pieces in plastic wrap and flatten to about 1 cm (1/2 inch) thick. Heat 25 g (3/4 oz) butter and 1 tablespoon oil in a large pan. Cook the chicken in batches over moderate heat for 2–3 minutes each side, until cooked through. Remove from the pan and keep warm. Add 4 tablespoons lemon juice to the pan and simmer gently for

1 minute. Whisk in 50 g (1²/3 oz) butter in small pieces until combined. Meanwhile, steam, boil or microwave 24 fresh asparagus spears until tender but still crisp. Serve the asparagus with the chicken, drizzled with the sauce and topped with shavings of fresh Parmesan.
Ready to eat in 30 minutes. Serves 4

NUTRITION PER SERVE
Protein 40 g; Fat 25 g; Carbohydrate 2 g; Dietary Fibre 1.5 g; Cholesterol 135 mg; 1680 kJ (400 cal)

Chicken and Pasta Soup

Finely dice 2 chicken breast fillets, and roughly chop 1 cup (90 g/3 oz) mushrooms. Heat 2 tablespoons olive oil in a pan and cook 1 finely diced onion until soft and golden. Add the chicken, mushrooms, 180 g (5³/4 oz) dried broken-up pasta and 6 cups (1¹/2 litres) chicken stock. Bring to the boil. Reduce the heat and simmer for

10 minutes. Stir in 1 cup (35 g/1¹/4 oz) fresh basil leaves and season with ¹/2 teaspoon salt and freshly ground black pepper, to taste.
Ready to eat in 30 minutes. Serves 4

NUTRITION PER SERVE
Protein 25 g; Fat 15 g; Carbohydrate 35 g; Dietary Fibre 5 g; Cholesterol 40 mg; 1480 kJ (355 cal)

Note: This is quite a chunky soup. Add more stock if preferred.

From left to right: Roasted Chicken and Tomatoes with Rosemary; Asparagus Chicken; Chicken and Pasta Soup

Green Chicken Curry with Beans

*Ready to eat in
30 minutes
Serves 4*

1 tablespoon oil
1–2 tablespoons green
  curry paste
1¹/4 cups (310 ml/
  10 fl oz) coconut
  cream
¹/2 cup (125 ml/4 fl oz)
  water
8 chicken tenderloins,
  cut into bite-size
  pieces
150 g (5 oz) green
  beans, cut into short
  lengths
4 kaffir lime leaves
1 tablespoon fish sauce
1 tablespoon brown
  sugar
1 tablespoon lime juice
¹/3 cup (10 g/¹/4 oz)
  fresh coriander leaves

1. Heat the oil in a
wok. Add the green
curry paste and stir-fry
for 1–2 minutes. Pour
in the combined
coconut cream and
water. Bring to the boil
and simmer for
5 minutes.
2. Add the chicken,
beans and kaffir lime
leaves. Bring to the boil
and simmer for
10 minutes, or until the
chicken is cooked
through.
3. Stir in the fish sauce,
brown sugar, lime juice
and coriander leaves.
Serve at once.

NUTRITION PER SERVE
*Protein 35 g; Fat 20 g;
Carbohydrate 8 g; Dietary
Fibre 3 g; Cholesterol
110 mg; 1565 kJ (375 cal)*

Chicken with Prosciutto and Sun-dried Capsicum

*Ready to eat in
30 minutes
Serves 4*

4 chicken breast fillets
2 tablespoons olive oil
2 teaspoons lemon juice
¹/2 cup (80 g/2²/3 oz)
  sun-dried capsicum,
  sliced
4 slices (75 g/2¹/2 oz)
  prosciutto, chopped
¹/3 cup (50 g/1²/3 oz)
  pine nuts, toasted
¹/3 cup (20 g/²/3 oz)
  chopped fresh basil
12 pitted black
  olives

Dressing
¹/4 cup (60 ml/2 fl oz)
  light olive oil
1 tablespoon balsamic
  vinegar
1 teaspoon Dijon
  mustard
¹/2 teaspoon caster
  sugar

1. Slash the chicken
breast fillets and place
in a dish with
1 tablespoon of the oil
and the lemon juice.
Mix well.
2. Combine the
capsicum, prosciutto,
pine nuts, basil and
olives in a bowl.
3. To make Dressing:
Place the dressing
ingredients in a jar and
shake well to combine.
4. Heat a heavy-based
pan with the extra oil.
Cook the chicken for
3–4 minutes each side,
or until cooked
through. Brush often
with the marinade
during cooking. Cut
each fillet into
diagonal slices.
5. Place the sliced
chicken fillet onto a
warm serving plate.
Top with a portion of
the capsicum mixture,
then drizzle with the
Dressing. Serve warm.
Garnish with fresh
herbs if desired.

NUTRITION PER SERVE
*Protein 40 g; Fat 40 g;
Carbohydrate 3 g; Dietary
Fibre 1 g; Cholesterol
90 mg; 2160 kJ (515 cal)*

Note: Sun-dried
capsicums are
available at most good
supermarkets.

---

*Green Chicken Curry with Beans (top) with
Chicken with Prosciutto and Sun-dried
Capsicum*

Chicken, Potato and Bean Salad

*Ready to eat in
25 minutes*
Serves 4

500 g (1 lb) new
  potatoes, sliced
1 clove garlic, crushed
1/3 cup (80 ml/2 3/4 fl oz)
  extra virgin olive oil
1 tablespoon white
  wine vinegar
1 tablespoon whole egg
  mayonnaise
1 teaspoon Dijon
  mustard
1 bunch rocket
200 g (6 1/2 oz) baby
  green beans, topped,
  tailed and halved
200 g (6 1/2 oz) yellow
  beans, topped, tailed
  and halved
25 g (3/4 oz) butter
2–3 (500 g/1 lb)
  chicken breast fillets,
  chopped
2 tomatoes, finely diced
1 tablespoon tiny
  capers

1. Cook the potato in a large pan of boiling water until just tender; drain. Combine the garlic, oil, vinegar, mayonnaise and mustard in a bowl. Season with salt and pepper; set aside.
2. Meanwhile, arrange the rocket on a plate.
3. Plunge the beans into a large pan of boiling water and cook for 2 minutes. Cool in a bowl of iced water and drain. Heat the butter in a frying pan, add the chicken and cook until tender. Keep warm.
4. Combine the potato, chicken, beans and tomato and serve over the rocket. Drizzle with dressing, sprinkle with capers and serve.

NUTRITION PER SERVE
*Protein 35 g; Fat 30 g;
Carbohydrate 20 g; Dietary
Fibre 5 g; Cholesterol
80 mg; 2045 kJ (490 cal)*

Creamy Chicken with Pastry Shapes

*Ready to eat in
30 minutes*
Serves 4

50 g (1 2/3 oz) butter
2–3 chicken breast
  fillets (500 g/1 lb total
  weight), chopped
1 leek, finely sliced
1 tablespoon plain
  flour
3/4 cup (185 ml/6 fl oz)
  chicken stock
1/2 cup (125 ml/4 fl oz)
  cream
3/4 cup (65 g/2 1/4 oz)
  button mushrooms
1 sheet puff pastry
1 teaspoon Dijon
  mustard

1. Preheat the oven to moderately hot 200°C (400°F/Gas 6). Heat half the butter in a large pan. Add the chicken and cook until well browned. Set aside. Heat the remaining butter and add the leek. Stir until softened slightly, then cover. Allow the leek to sweat for 5 minutes.
2. Stir in the flour and cook for 1 minute. Remove from the heat and stir in the stock and cream. Return the chicken to the pan; return to the heat and continue stirring until the mixture boils and thickens. Reduce the heat. Simmer, covered, for 10 minutes. Slice the mushrooms and add to the pan. Cook for 5 minutes more.
3. Meanwhile, cut the pastry into shapes of your choice using pastry cutters. Place on a baking sheet and cook in the oven for 12 minutes, until puffed and golden.
4. Add the mustard to the chicken; season to taste with sea salt and black pepper. Place in a serving dish and top with the pastry shapes.

NUTRITION PER SERVE
*Protein 35 g; Fat 35 g;
Carbohydrate 20 g; Dietary
Fibre 2 g; Cholesterol
150 mg; 2225 kJ (530 cal)*

*Chicken, Potato and Bean Salad (top)
and Creamy Chicken with Pastry Shapes*

Sautéed Chicken Livers with Pancetta

*Ready to eat in
  30 minutes
Serves 4*

1 tablespoon olive oil
25 g (3/4 oz) butter
50 g (1 2/3 oz) pancetta,
  chopped (see Note)
5 spring onions, finely
  sliced
500 g (1 lb) chicken
  livers, trimmed, cut
  into bite-sized pieces
1 teaspoon flour
2 cloves garlic, crushed
1/3 cup (80 ml/
  2 3/4 fl oz) wine
1 tablespoon balsamic
  vinegar
2 teaspoons Dijon
  mustard
3 tablespoons finely
  chopped fresh parsley
mixed salad leaves, to
  serve

1. Heat the olive oil
and butter in a large
frying pan. Add the
pancetta and cook over
moderate heat until
golden. Add the spring
onions and cook
until softened.
2. Toss the chicken
livers in the flour, then
increase the heat and
add the livers and garlic
to the pan. Cook for
about 4 minutes, or
until browned. Remove
from the heat and stir
in the wine, balsamic

vinegar and Dijon
mustard.
3. Return to the heat
and stir until the
mixture boils and
thickens. Season with
salt and pepper. Stir in
the parsley. Serve with
the mixed salad leaves
and a couple of slices of
crusty bread.

NUTRITION PER SERVE
*Protein 25 g; Fat 30 g;
Carbohydrate 10 g; Dietary
Fibre 5 g; Cholesterol
600 mg; 1800 kJ (430 cal)*

Note: If pancetta is not
available, lean bacon
can be used instead.
If balsamic vinegar is
not available, add a
small amount of dark
brown sugar to red
wine vinegar.

Oriental Chicken Stir-fry

*Ready to eat in
  30 minutes
Serves 4*

250 g (8 oz) dried thin
  egg noodles
1 barbecue chicken
1 tablespoon oil
1 onion, sliced
1 clove garlic, crushed
100 g (3 1/2 oz) baby
  corn
1 red capsicum, sliced
100 g (3 1/2 oz) sugar
  snap peas

1 bunch asparagus, cut
  into short lengths
1/4 cup (60 ml/2 fl oz)
  sweet chilli sauce
2 tablespoons lime juice
2 tablespoons soy
  sauce

1. Cook the noodles in
a large pan of boiling
water for 6 minutes, or
until tender. Drain and
set aside. Remove the
skin and bones from
the chicken and shred
the flesh.
2. Heat the oil in a
wok. Add the onion
and cook 1–2 minutes.
Stir in the garlic and
cook for 1 minute. Add
the corn, capsicum,
sugar snap peas and
asparagus and toss over
medium-high heat for
3–4 minutes.
3. Add the chicken and
noodles to the wok and
toss to combine. Add
the sweet chilli sauce,
lime juice and soy sauce
to the pan and stir
through. Serve
immediately.

NUTRITION PER SERVE
*Protein 40 g; Fat 20 g;
Carbohydrate 65 g; Dietary
Fibre 2.5 g; Cholesterol
165 mg; 2610 kJ (625 cal)*

Note: Egg noodles
are made from egg
and wheat flour and
are widely available.

*Sautéed Chicken Livers with Pancetta (top)
with Oriental Chicken Stir-fry*

Index